Most Popular
Arctic & Antarctic Animals

Billy Grinslott & Kinsey Marie Books

ISBN - 9781965098622

Arctic lemmings turn white in the winter to blend into the land of snow and ice. Arctic Lemmings build nests under the permafrost to help survive the cold winters. Lemmings build runway systems beneath rocks and underground. Lemmings eat plants like mosses, grasses, herbs, shoots, and algae. Arctic foxes are predators of lemmings, but lemmings can be hard to catch because they burrow deep into the snow. Most Arctic Lemmings don't survive more than one winter in the wild, because the harsh conditions.

Arctic ground squirrels are the largest ground squirrel in North America. During the cold temperatures, they can spend up to nine months in hibernation. They are the only known vertebrate that can survive body temperatures that drop below freezing while hibernating. They store food in their burrows during the summer for use in the spring when they wake up from hibernation. They are part of the Sciuridae family, which includes marmots, chipmunks, and prairie dogs. They are one of the only squirrels that can survive frigid temperatures.

The Stoat is part of the weasel family. Stoats can thrive in many climates and environments. They can live in most habitats if there's food and shelter. Stoats are opportunistic predators that hunt day and night. They have a strong sense of smell and can travel up to 1.5 miles in a few hours. Stoats are good at climbing trees. They can swim and dive underwater. Stoats can reach speeds of up to 20 miles an hour. In colder climates, stoats turn almost completely white, with just a black tip on their tail.

The Arctic hare survives the cold temperatures with a thick coat of fur. The black fur on the ears keeps its ears warm when the sun is shining. They have black eyelashes which protect its eyes from sun glare during the winter. Arctic hares are larger than rabbits. They have taller hind legs and longer ears. Arctic hares can run up to 40 miles an hour. In winter, they sport a brilliant white coat that provides excellent camouflage in the land of ice and snow.

A wolverine's color patterns are unique. No wolverine has the same fur color as another. Wolverines don't hibernate in the winter. They sleep in caves, rock crevices, or under fallen trees. Wolverines have a keen sense of smell that can detect another animal 20 feet under the snow. Wolverines have poor eyesight and are active at night. Wolverine babies are called kits. They are born with white fur that turns brown as they age.

The Lynx is larger than the bobcat and has lighter fur and more spots. The lynx is more than twice the size of a house cat. Lynx have natural snowshoes for feet because they have long hair on their feet. Lynx like to hunt at night. They have excellent hearing and eyesight, and can spot a mouse from 250 feet away. Lynx have colors that help them blend into their surroundings. Each lynx has a different pattern, similar to a human fingerprint.

The arctic fox with its thick fur can endure temperatures that reach -90 degrees. Being able to survive in such cold weather makes it a great animal for living on the Arctic tundra and pack ice. The arctic fox does not hibernate, their fur changes colors with the seasons. The Arctic fox is the smallest member of the dog family, it's about the size of a large house cat. They live in burrows, with extensive tunnel systems.

Arctic wolves have two thick layers of fur. The outer layer gets thicker in the winter months. As a result, their body temperature can stay warm enough even when it is bitter cold outside. Arctic wolves have white fur all year which allows them to blend into their snowy surroundings. They have fur on the paws to insulate them from snow and ice and it also provides for a better grip on slippery surfaces. Arctic wolves have keen senses of sight, hearing, and smell. Arctic wolves live in packs of just a couple members to about twenty.

Needing insulation from Arctic temperatures, snowy owls have a lot of feathers. This makes them one of the heaviest owls in North America. Their feet are covered with feathers, like fluffy little slippers. Their wingspan is 4 to 5 feet on average. The Arctic summer forces snowy owls to live in the daylight. Unlike most owls that are nocturnal and come out at night. Snowy owls are often seen during the daylight.

Arctic terns migrate between the Arctic and Antarctica, traveling more than 25,000 miles each year. This is the longest migration route of any bird. Arctic terns often return to the same area where they were born. Arctic terns can live up to 35 years, which is long for birds. Arctic terns molt in the winter, losing their feathers and growing new ones. During this time, they rarely fly. Arctic terns have a variety of calls, including an alarm call. Arctic terns are sometimes called the swallow of the sea because of their long tail feathers that split apart like a swallows tail.

Ptarmigans have dense plumage and feathered feet that allow them to walk on snow and roost in snowbanks. They change color from brown in summer to white in winter. Ptarmigans live in the subarctic tundra and high mountains. They are well-suited to cold winters, using snow burrows for shelter. Ptarmigans are game birds that are slightly larger than a grey partridge. The best place to find them is Alaska.

Yellow-billed loons are black with white spots on their backs and light-yellow bills. Yellow-billed loons are among the world's best diving birds, able to stay underwater for over a minute. Yellow-billed loons are strong fliers, reaching speeds of up to 40 mph. They use rapid wingbeats to fly. Unlike most birds, loons have solid bones that make them less buoyant and better at diving. Yellow-billed loons live in Arctic tundra habitats and winter along the coastlines of the Bering Sea and Aleutian Islands. They are also known as White-billed Divers.

Tundra swans migrate in family groups, flying in a V formation. They can fly as fast as 50 miles per hour. Tundra swans form strong pair bonds that may last for years. They are very social and interact often with other swans within their groups. Tundra swans are known for their whistling calls and their wings make a whistling noise when they fly, so many people call them whistling swans. The Tundra swan is a strong swimmer and can take off from the water with a running start and beat their wings until airborne. Juvenile tundra swans are called cygnets.

Male bluethroats have a striking blue throat with red or white centers, bordered by black and chestnut bands. They also have a reddish-brown tail. Bluethroats are secretive and hard to see but are more visible when singing or flying. Male bluethroats have a loud, varied song that they often sing from a perch or while flying. They also mimic the songs of other birds. Bluethroats can mimic the calls of up to 40 different bird species. Bluethroats live in wet birch wood or bushy swamps in Alaska.

Thick-billed murres are among the deepest divers of all birds, reaching depths of over 330 feet. They use their wings to fly underwater, and their feet for steering. Most birds fly to migrate, but Thick-billed murres migrate by swimming to their wintering grounds. The migration can cover up to 600 miles, that's a long way to swim. They are one of the most abundant marine birds in the Northern Hemisphere. They thrive in cold waters.

Snow Geese make epic journeys by air, but they are impressive on foot, too. Within the first three weeks of hatching, goslings may walk up to 50 miles with their parents from the nest to a more suitable feeding area. Snow geese migrate to the tundra of Canada and Alaska. Snow geese fly in large flocks, both during the day and night, and often return to the same nesting area each year. Snow geese are very vocal and can be heard from more than a mile away. They use vocalizations to communicate with each other. Snow geese are strong fliers, walkers, and swimmers. Snow geese are one of the world's most abundant waterfowl species.

Common eiders are the largest duck species in the Northern Hemisphere. It's a true sea duck, rarely found away from coasts. Eiders are famous for their down feathers, which they use to line their nests to keep eggs warm and their feathers help keep them warm in freezing temperatures. People have used eider down feathers for over 1,000 years in clothing. Eiders can dive underwater up to 180 feet but prefer to forage in shallower waters. Eiders are sociable birds that often nest in colonies. Eiders have a special gland that allows them to process and drink salt water, unlike other birds and animals.

An albatross has the largest wingspan of any living bird, measuring up to 12 feet across. Albatrosses can fly for days without flapping their wings. They use wind currents to float in and let the wind carry them. Once they are in the wind current, they even sleep in the air while being carried by the wind current. Albatrosses can smell food in the water from 12 miles away. They spend 80% of their lives at sea and can live up to 60 years.

Snow petrels are pure white birds with jet black beaks and eyes. They are the size of a pigeon. Snow petrels are found in the cold areas around Antarctica, and hang around pack ice, and also live in colonies on cliffs and rock faces. Snow petrels are not well suited for long distance flights. Snow petrels have a gland above their nasal passage that excretes a saline solution to help them balance the amount of salt in their body. Snow petrels live farther south than any other bird, in the Antarctic.

Skuas are large, dark brown seabirds about the size of sea gulls. Skuas birds are also known as avian pirates, because they steal food from other birds. They are known to dive-bomb people who get too close to their nests. They live most of their lives at sea, and only come ashore during the Arctic summer. They are often seen flying low and fast above the waves in pursuit of food.

Antarctic shags are about 30 inches tall and weigh around 7 pounds. Antarctic shags don't migrate and stay in their habitats all year round. They are found in the South Shetland Islands, Elephant Island, and along the Antarctic Peninsula. They are often found close to pack ice in and live in large colonies. They build cone-shaped nests out of their feathers, seaweed, and general beach debris, all glued together with their poop, icky.

Atlantic puffins and Tufted puffins are nicknamed sea parrots or clowns of the see. Because their big orange beak looks like a parrots or clown's nose. Puffins spend most of their lives out at sea, resting on the waves. When flying, Puffins flap their wings up to 400 times a minute and fly up to 55 mph. Their feathers make them appear puffed up, that's how they got their name Puffins. A puffin's beak changes color during the year. But in spring it blooms with an outrageous orange color. Puffins spend most of their lives out at sea, resting on the waves.

White Sided Dolphins live in both the Pacific and Atlantic Oceans. They are the biggest species of dolphin in the North Pacific. They like to jump out of the water and do acrobatics while jumping. They like to travel in large groups. They are often seen with other whales and dolphins. They can hold their breath underwater for up to six minutes before surfacing for air. Pacific white-sided dolphins eat squid, and small fish, like sardines, herring, and capelin.

White-beaked dolphins are found in colder temperate and subpolar waters throughout the North Atlantic Ocean. White-beaked dolphins are active swimmers. They often breach and jump at the water's surface and will sometimes surf on the waves created by ships. They travel in groups of 5–50 but can also gather in groups of hundreds or thousands. Adults are usually 9 feet long and weigh 600 pounds. They often swim in mixed schools with other species of dolphins and whales. They eat fish, squid, octopus, and crustaceans.

The Hourglass Dolphin got its name because the white on their side narrows down like an hourglass. Hourglass dolphins are most commonly seen around the Antarctic Convergence, between South America and Macquarie Island. Hourglass dolphins are known for leaping through waves in front of ships. They are small to robust dolphins with short, stocky bodies and large dorsal fins. They can grow to be up to 6 feet long. They are the only small dolphin species found in Antarctic waters.

The Greenland shark is the world's longest living fish. It can live for 400 years, twice the age of the longest-living land animal, the giant tortoise. Most Greenland sharks are partly blind because of parasites that attach themselves to the cornea of the eyes of the sharks. The Greenland shark lives in the cold waters of the North Atlantic Ocean and the Artic Ocean. They can grow to be 24 feet long and weigh over 2,000 pounds. Their flesh is poisonous and can cause illness or even death in humans.

Weddell Seals live the furthest south of any mammals. Weddell Seals are the most studied of any Seal species in the Antarctic. Females are generally a little bit bigger than males. They live around Antarctica in the Southern Ocean. They keep breathing holes in the ice open by rasping back and forth with their teeth, this allows them to live in ice covered areas. They have large eyes that help them to search for food in the sea where light is limited under the ice. Weddell seals are impressive divers, they can dive 1900 feet and be underwater for 80 minutes.

Antarctic fur seals are mostly distributed in Subantarctic islands. Adult males are dark brown, and females and juveniles are gray with lighter undersides. Pups are black when born and turn to a silver-gray color when they are 2 to 3 months old. Antarctic fur seals are the only seals with visible ears that live in Antarctica. Antarctic fur seals nearly became extinct during the time of the 18th and 19th centuries. Now the Antarctic fur seals are the most abundant species of fur seal. There's an estimated population of 4 million seals.

Ringed Seals get their name from the circular rings on their fur coat. Ringed seals can live in areas that are completely covered with ice. They use their sharp claws to make and maintain their own breathing holes through the ice. The ringed seal is the smallest of all living seal species. It lives on the Arctic Sea ice and ocean. Female ringed seals create lairs for their pups in the sea ice surface, which provide protection from extreme weather and predators. Ringed seals swim about 6 miles per hour and dive to 300 feet.

The Bearded Seal got its name because of its long whiskers that looks like a beard. Bearded seals live in the Arctic and sub-Arctic regions. They are the largest seal species in the Arctic, reaching a maximum length of 8 feet and weight of 950 pounds. Bearded seal pups can swim and dive within hours of being born. Bearded seals are very vocal and create trill sounds that can be heard up to 12 miles away. Bearded seals use their claws to create breathing and swimming holes in the sea ice. Bearded seals can sleep vertically in the ocean with their heads just above the surface.

Leopard seals got their name because they have spots like a leopard. Leopard seals are the third largest seal in the world. Sometimes leopard seal's smile. Leopard seals sing underwater. They have been known to give fish to humans. Leopard seals sometimes play with their food like kids do. Leopard seals have been known to hold their breath for about 15 minutes while swimming. Leopard seals can grow to be 12 feet long and weigh over 1,300 pounds. Leopard seals live along the edge of Antarctica. They thrive in one of the most inhospitable habitats on Earth.

Crabeater seals do not actually eat crabs. Crabeater Seals have a unique adaptation for feeding. They have evolved a sieve-like tooth structure that filter krill. They suck in water containing krill, close their jaws, and then force the water back out between their specialized teeth, trapping the krill inside. Their name originates from the German word, Krebs, which covers other crustacea as well as crabs.

Elephant seals get their name because their nose is like an elephant's trunk. Male elephant seals weigh as much as a small truck or cargo van. Elephant seals spend up to 80% of their lives in the ocean. They can hold their breath for 100 minutes when swimming. They can swim 60 miles a day. Elephant seals live for just two months of the year on land. They are the largest seal in the world.

There are only 2 types of walruses, the Atlantic and Pacific. Both male and female walruses have long tusks. Mother walruses are very protective of their young. A walrus can live to be 40 years old. Walruses don't like swimming in deep water. Walruses rest on ice or on shore. Thick layers of blubber protect walruses from the cold arctic temperatures. Walruses weigh up to 1.5 tons, as much as some cars. Walruses can sleep in water. They are very sociable and like to hang out with their friends.

Brush-tailed penguins, have long, stiff feathers and tail feathers that resemble a brush. They are cold-water penguins that live in polar or subpolar oceans. They are skilled swimmers that use their wings like flippers and their tails like rudders. They are very acrobatic. They swim underwater, jump out of the water, fly through the air, and then dive back down. They normally grow to be about 30 inches tall. They are known for being highly social, and interacting with each other frequently.

Adelie's penguins build their nests with stones and are known to steal stones from other penguin nests. They are known to rock back on their heel and prop themselves up on land utilizing their tail feathers. Adelie Penguins are very faithful to their family and nest sites. When Adelie penguin chicks are about nine weeks old, their downy baby feathers have been replaced by waterproof adult feathers. They live in some of the coldest places on earth. They are the smallest penguin species in Antarctica, standing 18–24 inches tall and weighing 12 pounds.

The chinstrap penguin gets its name from the narrow black band under its head which makes it look like it's wearing a black helmet. This makes it one of the most easily identified types of penguins. The chinstrap penguin can withstand swimming in freezing waters due to its tightly packed feathers, which provide a waterproof coat. Chinstrap penguins are highly social birds, gathering in large colonies. They swim as far as 50 miles offshore every day to feed.

Ellsworth's gentoo penguins live exclusively on the coast of Antarctica. They look virtually identical to other gentoo penguins but are smaller. These gentoos have also adapted to live on gravelly beaches and the mouths of rocky glacial valleys on the Antarctic. An adult Gentoo Penguin makes as many as 450 dives a day foraging for food. They can remain underwater for up to seven minutes. Gentoo Penguins can swim up to 22 miles an hour.

The Macaroni Penguin is the most abundant species in the world. These penguins are also considered as one of the largest and heaviest. An average adult Macaroni penguin can reach up to 28 inches high and weigh about 12 lbs. They can dive down to 200 feet and can hold their breath for up to three minutes. Macaroni penguins live in rocky areas on cliffs above the ocean.

Rockhoppers are the smallest of the crested penguins. They have a thin yellow crest that extends behind their eyes. These penguins are very vocal, making loud calls to ward off unwelcome visitors. Rockhopper penguins are native to the colder parts of the world. They are the most widely distributed penguin species. They can't consume too much salt, or they get ill. They have glands above their eyes that secrete the salt, so it doesn't absorb into their system. Otherwise, they would get sick by swimming in the salt water.

King penguins don't build nests to lay eggs. They stand upright and incubate the egg on the tops of their feet under a loose fold of skin. The chicks hatch with no feathers and are dependent upon their parents until they grow them. King penguins are the second largest of the penguin species. King penguins have colorful feathers around their necks and heads, this makes them the brightest of all the species of penguin.

Emperor penguins are the world's largest penguins. Being big helps them stay warm. Emperor penguins can withstand the Antarctic winter, where temperatures can plunge to -60°F and winds can howl up to 124 mph. Emperor penguins may be the only birds to never set foot on land. They are entirely dependent on living on sea ice. They hug to stay warm.

The narwhal has a long tusk on its face. Their tusk can grow as long as ten feet. They spend their lives in the cold Arctic waters and change color with age. They can dive as deep as 4,500 ft. Narwhal whales can spend more than three hours a day underwater, before coming up for air. They use their tusks for spearing fish and breaking ice.

Bowhead Whales can grow up to 60 feet long and weigh over 200,000 pounds. while still being able to leap out of the water. Bowhead whales can live to be over 200 years old, making them some of the longest-living mammals on Earth. Bowhead whales have the thickest blubber, layer of fat, of all the whales. Bowhead whales are the only whales to live exclusively in the Arctic. Bowhead whales are creative singers with many different songs. Their skull can be over 16.5 feet long, about a third of their body length. Bowhead whales can break through sea ice that is at least 2 feet thick using their large skulls and powerful bodies.

Orcas, known as killer whales, are the largest member of the dolphin family. A male orca can be 32 feet in length and weigh 22 thousand pounds, as big as a school bus. Orcas are intelligent and able to coordinate maneuvers. Orcas are extremely fast swimmers. Orcas are skilled hunters that coordinate their attacks in packs, like wolves. Orcas live in every ocean in the world. Orcas communicate with each other using clicks, whistles, and pulsing calls. They sleep with one eye open and can see any other fish coming their way.

Fin whales can grow up to 85 feet long and weigh 72 tons. Fin whales are the second largest whales in the world, after blue whales. Fin whales are the fastest great whales, swimming up to 23 miles per hour. Fin whales can live up to 90 years. Fin whales have accordion-like throats that help them gulp up to 4,000 pounds of food a day. Fin whales are fast swimmers and are known to raise their heads above the water, while swimming. They are found throughout the world's oceans.

Sperm whales are the largest of all toothed whales and can grow to a maximum length of 52 feet and weight of 90,000 pounds. Sperm whales have the largest brain of any living animal, weighing up to 9 pounds. Sperm whales are the deepest diving marine mammals, able to dive to depths of more than 3,000 ft. The longest recorded dive for a sperm whale was more than 2 hours.

Minke whales are the smallest of the great whales, growing to about 35 feet long and weighing up to 20,000 pounds. Minke whales can stay submerged for at least 15 minutes before returning to the surface for air. Minke whales live up to 50 years. Minke whales are the most common of the great whale species and can be found throughout the world's oceans.

Humpback whales grow up to 60 feet long and weigh 80,000 pounds. Humpback whales can live for 90 years. Humpback whales have some of the longest migrations of any mammal with some swimming 5,000 miles. Humpback whales eat up to 3,000 pounds of food a day. Humpback whales create and sing songs that can be heard up to 20 miles away. Humpback whales are named for the distinctive hump on their backs.

The beluga whale is easily recognizable thanks to its stark white coloring and globular head. Belugas are very social animals, and it's possible to see pods numbering in the hundreds. Beluga whales are one of the most vocal of all whales. Belugas are social animals that use clicks, whistles, chirps, and squeals to communicate. These white whales are born dark gray. It can take up to eight years before they turn completely white. The beluga can change the shape of its forehead, by blowing air around its sinuses. It's head will puff up. Belugas can live up to 50 years.

Dall sheep are the northernmost wild sheep in the world. The body of Dall sheep is covered with a white woolly coat that provides protection against low temperatures. Both males and females have horns. They are curved and tan in color. Their horns take up to 8 years to grow. The age of the sheep can be calculated from the number of growth rings on their horns. Dall sheep spend most of their lives on the jagged slopes of mountains. Their cloven hooves with rough pads help them cling to cliff edges and broken ledges.

There are six different subspecies of moose. Moose are built for cold areas and like living in cold regions with snow. Moose are the largest members of the deer family. Moose are huge and weigh up to 1500 pounds. Moose love water and are good swimmers. Moose have poor eyesight but compensate with a good sense of smell and hearing. At 5 days old they can outrun a person.

Caribou are also known as reindeer. Both male and female reindeer grow antlers. They are strong swimmers and can swim up to six miles per hour. Reindeer are covered in hair from their nose to the bottom of their hooves. Their fur color depends on where they live, with lighter colors in the north and darker colors in the south. They have large, hollow hooves that help them walk on snow and dig for food. Reindeer have hair completely covering their nose. Reindeer are the only deer species to be widely domesticated. Santa uses Reindeer to pull his slay. Rudolph the reindeer is the most popular of the reindeer.

The musk ox gets its name from the strong, musky smell that they release. These mammals have a double coat of fur to keep them warm. Musk oxen are native to the Arctic and are well-adapted to living in the frozen tundra. Musk ox are very smart animals. They're related to sheep and goats. Musk Ox use their strong hoofed feet to dig into the icy ground for grass and plants growing on the frozen tundra. Musk oxen live in groups called herds. When threatened, musk oxen gather in a circle with their heads facing out. Their babies are protected in the middle of the circle.

Brown bears are often called Grizzley bears, but they're not. Brown bears can be up to seven feet tall and weigh up to 700 pounds for males and 350 pounds for females. Brown bears eat mostly grass, roots, and berries but will eat fish and other small mammals. They are commonly silent but can communicate with grunts, roars, or squeals.

The Polar Bear is one of the biggest bears on earth. Male polar bears can weigh up to 1500 lbs. Female polar bears weigh about half as much as males. They like swimming and can swim constantly for days at a time. Polar bears keep warm thanks to the blubber or fat layer under their skin. They can smell up to a mile away. Polar bears spend most of their time at sea. They can run 25 mph, and they can swim up to 10 mph. There's still a debate of whether the Kodiak bear or the polar bear is the biggest bear in the world. Polar bears are found in Alaska and arctic areas.

Author Page

Billy Grinslott & Kinsey Marie Books

ISBN – 9781965098622

Thanks

www.ingramcontent.com/pod-product-compliance
Lightning Source LLC
Chambersburg PA
CBHW060822270326
41931CB00002B/57